Divine Quotes

Divine Quotes

Wistler W. Charles

All quotes in this book were written by Wistler W. Charles.
Cover design of the book was done by Wistler W. Charles.

Printed in the United States of America

To order additional copies of this book, contact:
Xlibris Corporation
1-888-795-4274
www.Xlibris.com
Orders@Xlibris.com
64715

Dedication

This book is lovingly dedicated:

To my Lord and Savior Jesus Christ

who has truly given me divine life. I could not imagine
where I would be without him being in my life.

Samantha

My darling wife who has always believe in my God given gifts and
talents.
Thanks for taking the time to type all of the quotes.

Joshuel

My precious son who expresses true love to me daily and makes me feel
like a true father.

Franco

My wonderful brother both in the flesh and in the Lord.
No one has pushed me to publish this book like my dear brother,
he truly believes in my abilities.

Apostle Paul Butler and Elder Maxine Butler

My pastors and teachers in the faith. Everything I have learned
about living victoriously in this world and in the
kingdom of God I have learned from you all.
This book is a reflection of all you have taught me over the years.

Alonzo Ford

My fellow soul winner who always took the time to listen to my quotes
and one who understood my desire to share the wisdom of God.

꧁ ꧂

1. "The greatest of opportunities is not the ones we create for ourselves,
    nor is it the opportunities that people create for us,
    but it is those opportunities that God creates for us."

2. "Opportunities do not always come gift wrapped."

3. "No one can reach their ultimate potential
    if they are in the wrong environment."

4. "God can make use of anything we give to Him."

꧁ ꧂

⁓

5.   "God can do great things with small things."

6.   "You can only accomplish your purpose with your God given talents."

7.   "A godly connection will produce a godly affection."

8.   "Great leaders will gather great followers to accomplish great things."

⁓

9. "If you cannot keep your word, you cannot keep anything, for as your word goes out of your mouth, so will everything go out of your life."

10. "Whatever someone loves, that is what they will cling to."

11. "Do not force anyone to leave what they love."

12. "Do not diminish what you have never replenished."

13. "Your success may take you high as the stars,
but pride will bring you down to the dust."

14. "Wherever you go in life, God is already there."

15. "Go where you can grow."

16. "Life is filled with warning signs which
we seldom pay any attention to."

⁓⊙℮ ℮⊙⁓

17. "When we fulfill our goals, we look for more challenges."

18. "Ordinary is ordinary to the ordinary person."

19. "When we subject our minds to worry,
we discard our faith for unbelief."

20. "He who backs out in times of challenges,
will never experience the joys of victory."

⁓⊙℮ ℮⊙⁓

21. "What we abandon, someone else will lay claim to."

22. "What we love, we treasure and what we treasure, we add value to."

23. "Appreciate someone and they will respect you,
respect someone and they will commend you at all times."

24. "When we underestimate people, we seldom give
them the respect and the prize they deserve."

❧❧ ❧❧

25. "Give people their highest value, and
they will give you your highest respect."

26. "Applause is not given to someone who has done something,
but it is given to the person who has done their best."

27. "Do not seek approval if you have not demonstrated excellence."

28. "Only accept defeat if you did not expect victory."

❧❧ ❧❧

ഗ⊘ ⊘ഖ

29. "Your dreams for your life may come while you are asleep,
but they must come to reality while you are awake."

30. "It's an honor to be given responsibility and a joy to fulfill it."

31. "Problems are not strange, they are normal."

32. "God has given all of mankind gifts, yet few of us accept them."

ഗ⊘ ⊘ഖ

ಀಀಀ ಀಀಀ

33. "What you accept in this world becomes a part of your life."

34. "If you refuse a life of mediocrity, you will gain a life of excellence."

35. "We add value to our life when we take away mediocrity from it."

36. "We become good-for-nothing when we are satisfied with where we are."

ಀಀಀ ಀಀಀ

ഔൟ ൟൟ

37. "Life is not about moments, but rather it's about momentum."

38. "Expect disappointments when you compromise your values."

39. "Half-way is not too far from all-the-way."

40. "In-between bad and excellent is mediocrity."

ഔൟ ൟൟ

41. "God is not common."

42. "There is always a common place for common ideas,
     but the uncommon idea must create its own place."

43. "Be careful of where you're always accepted,
    and keep in your heart where you're always rejected."

44. "Common and uncommon are not identical twins,
    in fact they are not even related."

45. "Common ideas are like plastic, if you stretch it to long it will tear."

46. "Ingenious ideas are the birth place for great innovations."

47. "When you become productive, you will always discover something new."

48. "We are all construction workers, for we are either helping construct our own life or someone else's life."

49. "Innovate to inspire and inspire to be innovative."

50. "The creative mind is always conceiving new ideas."

51. "Innovators stay ahead of the race and those who inspire is always ready to take the lead."

52. "New ideas are untried-so be the first."

53. "Don't conform to the common way of doing things, unless you want to do things the common way."

54. "The uncommon idea always seems unreal."

55. "Excellence is not far from good and good is not far from bad."

56. "Champions master the basics first."

ঞৈল গ্ঠ

57. "Failure can be easily predicted when we have not first mastered the basics."

58. "If we progress each day, we are bound to meet success."

59. "Defeat is sure when we think there is no need to do no more."

60. "Failure comes to the person who makes no effort to better themselves."

ঞৈল গ্ঠ

61. "If you surrender to your failures, they will keep you bound for a long time."

62. "Success comes when you have over-taken your failures."

63. "Don't catch up to your failures, overtake them."

64. "Failure controls, but good success brings freedom."

෴ ෴

65. "Failure is always in reverse."

66. "When there are setbacks, don't give up and don't give in, just start again."

67. "If you keep mastering what you do, victory will soon come to you."

68. "Do not wait too late to cry out for help."

෴ ෴

෴ඔ ඔ෴

69. "Doubt is like a hole in a boat, eventually the boat will sink."

70. "The longer you wait to help someone, the more help they will need."

71. "If you can't help yourself, then you need help."

72. "Know those who can help you."

෴ඔ ඔ෴

৵৹৹ ৹৹৹

73. "A person, who can help you in time of need, is more important than one thousand persons who can't help you at all."

74. "What may be important to you, may be the least of worries to others."

75. If you're filling your life with what is trivial, you're also emptying your life of that which is important."

76. "Leave where you are to go where you have never been before."

৵৹৹ ৹৹৹

⚬⚬⚬

77. "Great men do not stop people from doing great things."

78. "If you can't carry someone in your hands,
then carry them in your heart."

79. "Don't look for opportunities, create them."

80. "When we miss an opportunity to do good,
we miss an opportunity to get a divine blessing from God."

⚬⚬⚬

81. "Every good thing we do is a seed we plant,
   to reap a good harvest in the future."

82. "Your failures will put your life in reverse, but it's up
   to you to change the gear and put it in forward."

83. "Whether you fail or succeed, you will still learn something new."

84. "When you fail, you learned that you didn't succeed,
   and when you succeed, you learned that you didn't fail."

⁓ ⁓

85. "Knowledge has no power until you
     apply it effectively for the good of mankind."

86. "Purpose shows you the road to success,
     but determination is what helps you get there."

87. "A little fear can cut down the greatest of faith."

88. "The goal of fear is to make you believe
     the worst is going to happen to you."

⁓ ⁓

89. "Problems always expose our true strength."

90. "Problems are never overcome by fear, but by faith."

91. "Problems are no respecter of persons."

92. "Problems always show up without invitation."

93. "Problems have ears to hear,
so do yourself a favor and command them to leave."

94. "Words become what you want them to become."

95. "Words travel alone."

96. "Words are not blind, wherever you send it;
it will find its way and fulfill its purpose."

97. "Words without purpose always serve no purpose."

98. "Words become visible when we give them a task to fulfill."

99. "Words don't need friends."

100. "Man's greatest power is the words of his mouth."

101. "What you speak in faith shall be."

102. "Words get power when they are spoken in faith."

103. "Words are always at work, for our good or for our downfall."

104. "Words are always at work, yet seeks no wages,
only to give back what was given."

105. "When you understand your authority,
you will understand the authority of words."

106. "Words have the authority to become reality."

107. "Our words can go where our feet cannot take us."

108. "Words have power that cannot be seen with the naked eye."

109. "If life was a puzzle it would take a lifetime to put it together again."

110. "Parents fight many battles so their children can live in peace."

111. "Everyone's life is a book that is filled with interesting stories waiting to be read."

112. "Whatever you fill your life with you will always become thirsty off."

113. "There are no identical journeys in life."

114. "Perversity is a tree that bares the fruit of faithlessness."

115. "A man can never go forward in life
if his thinking is always in reverse."

116. "When your purpose and your thinking are in opposite
directions, your life will be filled with collisions."

117. "If you're not producing anything worthy in your life, then it makes no sense beginning anything new, unless it's something worthy."

118. "Change begins in the mind."

119. "When you focus only on what you have accomplished, you will lose the desire for what you can still achieve."

120. "Life is not about what you have but what you can produce."

⟳ ⟳

121. "Many live by the accomplishments of their forefathers,
but they themselves are producing nothing for the generations
that follows them to live by."

122. "What you have now is passing away, and if you
cease to be productive you will soon have nothing."

123. "We produce not to get more, but to replenish."

124. "A harmonious life is when it is constantly giving and producing."

⟳ ⟳

125. "A man will be lost in what he has
when he constantly gets but never gives."

126. "Do not talk of where you are going unless you
are prepared to change the way you are thinking."

127. "What you speak and what you think
are found on the same chain of what you do."

128. "When your history becomes more important than
your future, your present will have no meaning."

129. "A step backward to take a leap forward is
a characteristic of development."

130. "Change is not always taking a step forward,
but sometimes it's taking a step backward."

131. "A person who wants to change will manifest it,
not only with words but also with action."

132. "If someone has no regrets, they will have no desire to change."

∽ಲ ಲൡ

133. "A better life begins with you being sorry where
you are and happy of where you are going."

134. "Each step you make in life must accompany you changing
your thinking to accommodate your new position."

135. "To advance in anything, you have to advance in your thinking."

136. "To develop is to change, to change is to develop."

∽ಲ ಲൡ

⚜

137. "Taking your history into your future is like
taking a heavy load on your shoulder."

138. "Your history is better off in one place, that place is history."

139. "You cannot start something new,
if you're not first willing to change you."

140. "It's not only what you have done that changes
your thinking, but what you have not done."

⚜

༄༅ ༄༅

141. "You cannot produce what you have never sown."

142. "If you keep looking back at your past, you will
discover that someone has taken you over."

143. "Your past is a story, your present a sentence and your future a suspense."

144. "Pass achievements often hinder a person's future developments."

༄༅ ༄༅

⚬⚬⚬

145. "A person is slowly losing his life when he is not progressing in life."

146. "It is as if life gets rid of those that are not producing what is good for the good of mankind."

147. "What is not good lies in wait for those who refuse to do what is good."

148. "When you have too much, it means someone else has too little."

⚬⚬⚬

149. "Heaven is always open to those who are willing to pray."

150. "If a person does not feed their spirit, they
will never experience life in its fullest."

151. "A person will easily be attached to many things in his lifetime,
but when it's time to be separated from them, it will be a struggle."

152. "You can tell where a person is going
by the instructions they are following."

୬୧ୠ ୬ୠ୧

153. "We surrender quickly to life's problems when
we fail to accept God's answers to our problems."

154. "To say no to good instructions is to say yes to death."

155. "To follow a worthy instruction is to keep you living,
without it you will fade away."

156. "It is easy to break free from other people habits, but hard to
break free when we are under the influence of our own habits."

୬୧ୠ ୬ୠ୧

⚬⚬⚬

157. "It is easier to be loose by the words people trap us with, than by our own words which we trap ourselves with."

158. "Be careful what you speak out of your mouth, for you are either laying a trap for yourself or a way of escape."

159. "A person words are either a key or a lock."

160. "A person does not always trap themselves by what they see, but they often trap themselves by what they speak."

⚬⚬⚬

161. "Prison bars may keep a man in a cell,
but his own words may sentence him to a life of hell."

162. "The state you are in can often be traced
back to the words that came from your mouth."

163. "A person lays their own trap with their own words."

164. "A person plans their own capture with their own words."

165. "A few negative words today can lead to a lifetime of trouble."

166. "The opportunity to free yourself from bondage does come around often, so do it as soon as possible."

167. "Humility plus apology are two keys that unlock the doors of liberty."

168. "If you can free yourself, then free yourself."

169. "Never delay to be free."

170. "Apologies set for tomorrow may be a day too late."

171. "Apologies and humility wears out with every passing minute, so never delay to do them."

172. "Friendship is often loss with words and can be won back with words."

173. "Money is not a durable solution to poverty,
as it come so does it goes and poverty still lingers on."

174. "The poor remains poor because they
make poverty stronger than money."

175. "No one can fully release their potential until they
have helped someone fully release their potential."

176. "If you help someone up, then they will be able to pull you up."

෧ଇ ୨ଚ

177. "If you climb the ladder of success alone,
then you will be alone at the top."

178. "The success that brings joy is not the one that is celebrated alone,
but the one that is enjoyed with people who help bring about that
success."

179. "If the truth could die it would have many killers."

180. "The truth has few friends and many enemies."

෧ଇ ୨ଚ

181. "Some men see where they are going and
some see where they need to be."

182. "The only thing that can silence accusations is silence."

183. "Serve a leader and leaders will serve you."

184. "God has already given everyone what they
need to help someone else succeed."

⚜

185. "It is not always where we are that has what we need to succeed, it is usually found in the places where we fear to venture into."

186. "We learn to lead when we learn to serve."

187. "He, who serves well, will lead well."

188. "If we live life knowing that everything we need has been given to us by God, we will be more thankful, grateful and courageous."

⚜

189. "Follow to serve, serve to lead."

190. "Good success is not something to attain, it is something to receive."

191. "Leaders lead people to possess what is already theirs."

192. "Success is not a goal, it's a gift."

ৰৄ৫ ৭৶৹

193. "Life is filled with obstacles beware not to crossover them alone."

194. "Obstacles never show you what's behind you;
they only show what's in front of you."

195. "Some obstacles are there for you to go over,
some to go under and others to go through."

196. "A leader not only knows what is going on in them,
but also what is going on around them."

ৰৄ৫ ৭৶৹

⚜

197. "A leader is becoming a new person
when they are beginning something new."

198. "A leader leads effectively by following principles."

199. "Principles are the road map of life, detour from them
and you will find yourself lost in this world."

200. "Principles are the keys to prosperity."

⚜

꒰ಶ꒱ ꒰ಶ꒱

201. "People often forget what is common
when something new begins to evolve."

202. "No man can build his life alone, and his greatest quest
is to find the best people that can help him achieve this."

203. "It seems to me that all people were unassembled,
and it will take a team of people to assemble each one of us."

204. "He who does not improve his life will soon become extinct."

꒰ಶ꒱ ꒰ಶ꒱

205. "Life is like a marriage, but it's up to you
to accept the invitation to attend it."

206. "Winners are those people who purpose in their hearts
to help make other people winners."

207. "Where you are determines what happens to you."

208. "The quicker a person change their thinking,
the quicker their habits will change."

209. "When we focus only on ourselves, we will not celebrate with someone else's accomplishments."

210. "We make light of things that are not important to us."

211. "Life is an invitation, so do not reject it."

212. "To accomplish anything great, you must sacrifice to prepare and prepare to sacrifice."

⚜

213. "Don't forget where you came from and
remember where you are going."

214. "One will always same out of place
when they are not walking in their purpose."

215. "A person who does not know where they are in life
will always be out of place wherever they go."

216. "A person heart is fully exposed in times of showing love."

⚜

⚜

217. "Knowledge may not produce an experience,
but an experience will produce knowledge."

218. "What a man is not looking for he may find,
and what he is looking for he may not find."

219. "Life is the beginning of possibilities, but they
that are born often bring death to them."

220. "When we put value on what is meaningless,
we lose sight of that which is important."

⚜

✥

221. "Everything is not valuable, but everything is important."

222. "Place worth on everyone you come in contact with, and you will discover that you are priceless beyond measure."

223. "A leader does not know where he is going when he is pointing his followers to worthless paths."

224. "Slavery only flourishes where truth has no preeminence."

✥

෯ଵୄ ଵୄ෯

225. "No one is totally free until they are
totally free from the enslavement of sin."

226. "One must be discipline to live by principles,
and must live by principles to be discipline."

227. "Principles are not locks they are keys."

228. "If a person removes principles from their lives,
they will be moved by anything."

෯ଵୄ ଵୄ෯

꧁ ꧂

229. "Principles don't only take you through the
world, they make you valuable to the world."

230. "You are nothing until you begin living by principles."

231. "You cannot tell someone who they are
until you first discover who you are."

232. "A little help is sometimes better than great instructions."

꧁ ꧂

⁂

233. "No one can prepare for anything without the aid of knowledge."

234. "Knowledge always precedes preparation."

235. "When people have no knowledge of the challenges they are facing, they will have no knowledge on how to overcome it."

236. "Knowledge feeds the mind, but its wisdom that keeps it healthy."

⁂

237. "To prepare for anything without knowledge
is like going to war without weapons."

238. "I'd rather be armored with knowledge and wisdom,
than to be armored with weapons of destruction."

239. "I'd rather know the truth about my future
than the truth about my past."

240. "The truth does not always produce good feelings,
but it always sets you free."

241. "It's not the responsibility of knowledge to take us through the world, but it is our responsibility to take knowledge through the world."

242. "Knowledge only becomes a burden when our minds are not prepared to bear it."

243. "One must always make room in their mind for new knowledge by getting rid of old and useless knowledge."

244. "One cannot persuade someone to believe in them, if they have yet to believe in themselves."

245. "If a person does not learn to love from the heart,
they will not learn to forgive from the heart."

246. "To help a fellow man find freedom is the greatest act of
kindness, and to help him find himself is the greatest act of love."

247. "Love bears two fruit-the fruit to give and the fruit to forgive."

248. "We all have the authority to forgive, but few use that authority."

❧❧ ❧❧

249. "Live to give and love to forgive."

250. "No one starts to live until he starts to give."

251. "Giving comes from the hands of love,
and forgiving comes from the heart of love.

252. "The true virtue of living is the act of giving
and the true virtue of giving is the act of loving."

❧❧ ❧❧

253. "Forgiveness is the key that sets anyone free."

254. "Giving and forgiving yields the greatest returns of love."

255. "The thoughts of a man's heart are expressed by the words of his mouth."

256. "We all have the power to give love and to receive love."

ഏറ ഉപ

257. "God gets glory when we give away the love he has given us."

258. "A person discovers their calling while they are working."

259. "If you have answers, people with problems
will find you even if you are lost."

260. "Freedom is not a want, it's a need."

ഏറ ഉപ

261. "There are those who think they will find freedom by keeping others bound, but little that they know that finding freedom for themselves begins with freeing those that are bound."

262. "Accusers are not in a quest to find answers, but are in hot pursuit to find problems."

263. "Silence is sometimes a good answer to questions that lead to no good."

264. "If you have given someone power over your freedom, know this also that you have given them power over your life."

꧁ ꧂

265. "If you don't know me, then you can't decide what's best for me."

266. "Love is first seen and then heard."

267. "True love has no arterial motives."

268. "There are those who see bad in the good that people do
and there are those who don't see neither good nor bad in anything,
in my opinion neither of these are deserving of sight."

꧁ ꧂

269. "If it's easy for you to love, then it will be easy for you to forgive."

270. "Love has no secrets to hide and no faults to be ashamed of."

271. "Love makes itself known not only by what it
says but also by what it does."

272. "Love never stays one place."

⚬⚬⚬

273. "Love goes where love lives."

274. "The greatest power that God has given to mankind is the power of love."

275. "Love is not a follower it's a leader."

276. "Love is always calling, but many choose not to answer."

⚬⚬⚬

277. "Love is always looking for followers,
not to make them leaders but to make them lovers."

278. "One act of love always touches the heart of many."

279. "The flames of love can never be put out by streams of hatred."

280. "Love heals, love cures, love mends and love builds broken lives again."

281. "The power of love forgives and the power of the truth sets us free."

282. "A new journey will bring new experiences
and new experiences a new story to tell."

283. "To help is to heal."

284. "The eyes of love always see the work of faith."

285. "There are people who look for ways to help,
and there are those who look for ways to hurt."

286. "Love needs no audience to perform well."

287. "Whether in light or darkness love will be seen."

288. "To love is to forgive, to forgive is to love."

289. "Love has no secrets and truth has no prisoners."

290. "Love never goes to sleep and love never goes away."

291. "Love has no wants and love has no needs."

292. "True love always finds its way back home."

❧ ☙

293. "Love works for everyone and never asks to be paid."

294. "Your good words may get a man's attention,
but your good works will get his allegiance."

295. "No heart and no mind is love proof."

296. "Love has nothing to prove, just something to do."

❧ ☙

297. "Love makes itself known to all."

298. "For love to enter your mind, it must first enter your heart."

299. "Love makes everything seems easy."

300. "Success comes slow to the person who wants to achieve it alone."

301. "If a man has not lost his common sense, he has lost nothing."

302. "If you want to learn you will be intelligent, and if you want to be intelligent, you must want to learn."

303. "Blind eyes cannot see nature, blind minds cannot see knowledge, but a blind heart cannot see anything."

304. "Everything happens for the sake of knowledge."

ᥱᆬᏨ Ꮰᥲᥱ

305. "Tomorrow may not bring good news, but it will bring new knowledge."

306. "Knowledge helps a man find his way
through the many pathways of life."

307. "One will never be lost if they allow truth to guide their intelligence."

308. "It is possible for one to be intelligent and not have truth,
but it is impossible for one to have truth and not be intelligent."

ᥱᆬᏨ Ꮰᥲᥱ

⁓꙰⁓

309. "The world moves when knowledge is applied,
and comes to a halt because of ignorance."

310. "There are three inseparable friends, Mr. Do not see,
Mr. Do not go and Mr. Do not do."

311. "Someone is always crying out for our help
but we often do not hear their voice. "

312. "If you need help, never just wait for it, but look for it,
go for it, most of all ask for it."

⁓꙰⁓

༺๏ୠ๏༻

313. "The person who is seeking to do everything themselves,
is only desiring to please themselves."

314. "Two hands can do many things, but two hands cannot do everything."

315. "The mouth does more work than the hand, but the hand
gets more work accomplished than the mouth."

316. "Every experience delivers a message few of us hear or understand."

༺๏ୠ๏༻

317. "It is the little things we overlook in our lives that will either help us grow or help us wither away."

318. "Little habits bring down the greatest of men."

319. "What makes you excel is not always what it takes to keep you excelling."

320. "Many people concern themselves about securing what they have and pay no attention to what they lack."

321. "My goal is to grow, but my passion is to keep growing."

322. "Success often hides what is really missing from our lives."

323. "It's not gravity that brings down the successful,
but their little folly that they refuse to let go of."

324. "The environment you choose to live in
may lack the very thing you need to keep living."

325. "Where you are now in life may not have what
it takes to take you where you want to go."

326. "Many people seek to understand where they want to be in the
future, but have no interest in learning where they are now."

327. "Success may shed a light on what you have,
but your environment will expose what you lack."

328. "If you change your environment you will change your development."

329. "Never plant yourself in an environment
until you discover what it produces."

330. "Where you plant yourself tells me what you will become."

331. "Everyone will one day plant themselves somewhere,
but many will bear no fruit."

332. "First choose where you want to grow, then where you want to go."

ༀ❧ ❧ༀ

333. "Lack does not stop growth, it stops development."

334. "Before you set to discover an answer to a problem,
take the time to discover its purpose; perhaps in discovering
its purpose you may discover the answer."

335. "Solutions to problems do not always satisfy everybody;
to some it's a relief to others it's another problem."

336. "If a person despises their life, the days they live will have no meaning."

ༀ❧ ❧ༀ

337. "We are all born into this world with an assignment, which we all will carry out whether we know it or not."

338. "A breath, a heartbeat that is what we all are."

339. "Many are at war with their problems, few are at peace with them and a great number never solve them."

340. "Big problems sometimes need a little answer."

❧❧ ❧❧

341. "If you are tired of loving, then it's not love."

342. "Hope is still powerful even when we have no strength."

343. "The answers we ask for do not always give us the comfort we need."

344. "Success comes with patience, but patience does not come with success."

❧❧ ❧❧

৵৹ℚ 𝕾৯৹

345. "Friends are not God, but God is a friend."

346. "We all are open targets for love to pierce through."

347. There is a rightful place for everybody,
but many of us are on the wrong path to finding it."

348. "A man may know the truth but will still live by his opinion."

৵৹ℚ 𝕾৯৹

❧❦ ❦❧

349. "Hope secures in times of trouble."

350. "Give man knowledge and he will no longer feel inferior."

351. "A closed-mind will have a closed life,
a life difficult to comprehend a life without victory."

352. "Never expect to be victorious over anything you refuse to understand."

❧❦ ❦❧

৵৹৻ ৻৹৵

353. "Love does not have hands but you can still feel its touch,
love does not have a mouth but you can still hear its words,
and love does not have a body but you can still feel its presence."

354. "Love is not shallow, it is deep, and love is not cold, it is warm."

355. "If you love God you will love yourself, if you love yourself
you will love people and if you love people you will love life."

356. "Love heals all hurts and eases all pains."

৵৹৻ ৻৹৵

357. "Love is a seed so sow it."

358. "Love can grow anywhere, so plant it and
love can shine anywhere, so light it."

359. "When everything dies love will still be living."

360. "Love gives everything it has to get everything it never had."

❧❧ ❧❧

361. "No two person progresses at the same pace,
so there is no need to envy anyone."

362. "Everyone knows when they have failed, it's a silent pain
only that person feels and that no one else sees."

363. "Change is seldom welcome with open arms
and often rejected by the majority."

364. "There is no room for earthly treasures in the grave,
nor for the things we have accomplished in this life."

365. "When God and man work together, the whole
universe benefits."

❧❧ ❧❧